CHRISTMAS
Jesus Is Born!

Written by
Marlyn Evangelina Monge, FSP

Illustrated by
Lisa M. Griffin

Pauline
BOOKS & MEDIA
Boston

Library of Congress Cataloging-in-Publication Data

Names: Monge, Marlyn, author. | Griffin, Lisa M., 1972- illustrator.
Title: Christmas : Jesus is born! / written by Marlyn Evangelina Monge, FSP ; illustrated by Lisa Griffin.
Description: Boston, MA : Pauline Books & Media, 2018.
Identifiers: LCCN 2018002850| ISBN 9780819816702 (hardcover) | ISBN 0819816701 (hardcover)
Subjects: LCSH: Jesus Christ--Nativity--Juvenile literature. | Christmas--Juvenile literature.
Classification: LCC BT315.3 .M66 2018 | DDC 232.92--dc22
LC record available at https://lccn.loc.gov/2018002850

Cover design by Mary Joseph Peterson, FSP

Illustrated by Lisa M. Griffin

Published by Pauline Books & Media, 50 Saint Pauls Avenue, Boston, MA 02130–3491

Printed in the U.S.A.

CJIB VSAUSAPEOILL5-710117 1670-1

www.pauline.org

Pauline Books & Media is the publishing house of the Daughters of St. Paul, an international congregation of women religious serving the Church with the communications media.

1 2 3 4 5 6 7 8 9   22 21 20 19 18

To my amazing nieces and nephews:
Gabriela, Cristian, Jonathan, Joseph,
María Amada, and Sofía Noel—each of you
is a gift from God. May you and all the children
who read this book come to discover, welcome, and love
the greatest gift this world has ever received: **Jesus!**

*"And the Word became flesh and lived among
us, and we have seen his glory, the glory as of
a father's only son, full of grace and truth."*

John 1:14

A very long time ago, God sent the Archangel Gabriel to a young woman who lived in a small town named Nazareth. The woman's name was Mary. The angel brought a very important message from God.

Approaching her, Gabriel said, "Hail, Mary. You are filled with grace. Do not be afraid. God loves you and wants you to be the mother of his Son. You will have a baby, and you will name him Jesus. He will be great. He will be the Son of God."

Surprised by everything the angel had said, Mary bowed her head and asked, "How can this happen? I am not married yet." She was engaged to be married to a man named Joseph.

The Archangel Gabriel replied, "This will happen through the power of God, Mary. The Holy Spirit will come to you. For nothing is impossible for God."

Mary raised her head and said, "I am God's servant. Let it happen to me as you have said."

At that moment, the Holy Spirit came upon Mary. Immediately, Jesus, God's Son, began to grow inside his mother.

Many months passed and shortly before Mary was due to give birth, the emperor called for a census.

"Mary, the emperor has ordered all people to go to the city of their ancestors to be counted," Joseph told his wife. "My family is from the city of Bethlehem. We will have to go there."

"Is the city far from Nazareth?" Mary asked.

"It will be at least a five-day walk," Joseph explained. "I know it won't be easy for you since the baby will be born soon, but we must go. It will be a long journey, but I will help you and keep you safe. You can ride our little donkey."

"God will be with us," Mary said.

The next day, the couple and their donkey began the journey. It was a difficult trip, but Mary and Joseph trusted God to help them.

Families from all over Israel had traveled to Bethlehem for the census, and the city was very crowded. Although Joseph knocked on door after door, no one had room for them to stay.

"Mary, there's one last place we can try," Joseph said as he headed to a door.

"Hurry, Joseph," Mary said urgently. "The baby is coming!"

When the innkeeper opened the door, he looked at Mary and Joseph and shook his head. "I'm sorry," he said. "There's no room for you here. My inn is full."

"Please sir, isn't there anywhere we could stay? My wife says the baby is about to be born!" Joseph explained.

Looking at the tired woman, the man told Joseph, "You can stay in the place where we keep our cows and other animals. At least it will be warm and dry."

Mary and Joseph looked at each other. "We'll stay there," Joseph told the innkeeper. "Thank you for your kindness."

When Mary and Joseph arrived at the dark stable, Joseph lit an oil lamp. It would have been cold if not for the warmth of the sleeping animals. Joseph cleaned out a space and made a bed of hay in a corner. The animals opened their eyes to watch as Mary and Joseph moved around the once quiet stable.

"Come, Mary," said Joseph, "let me help you lie down. You'll be more comfortable on the hay."

The animals looked on as Mary slowly got to her knees and then sat down on the sweet-smelling hay.

Soon a baby's cry filled the stable.

"He's here," Mary sighed, smiling at her baby. "Welcome to the world, little one."

Outside, a star—brighter than any other star anyone
had ever seen—shone directly over the stable. Jesus was
born!

Mary wrapped her beautiful Son in strips of soft cloth. She hugged and kissed him. Then she sang quietly to Jesus while Joseph put some fresh hay in the open box that usually held food for the animals. "It's not much, but at least the manger is clean," he said.

Mary laid baby Jesus in the manger. The animals all crept closer to see the newborn child. Looking at her baby, Mary prayed joyfully, "Thank you, Lord God, for sending us your Son! I trust in your promise that he is our Savior!"

While Mary, Joseph, and the animals gazed at Jesus, another amazing thing was happening on the hills outside the city walls.

There were shepherds who lived on the hills. They were watching their flocks of sheep. Suddenly a bright light filled the night sky.

"Look!" one of the shepherds pointed out. "It's a new star!" The other shepherds lifted their gaze. Even the sheep stopped eating to see what was happening.

Then an angel appeared to the shepherds. They were frightened at the sight. "Do not be afraid," the angel told them. "I bring good news of great joy for all people!"

The shepherds gathered to hear the important message. "This very night the Savior, your Messiah, has been born in Bethlehem," the angel said. "You will find him lying in a manger and wrapped in pieces of cloth."

Then many angels appeared, praising God. They filled the night with their beautiful song:

"Glory to God in heaven,
and peace to his people on earth."

After the angels left, one of the shepherds said, "We must go to Bethlehem at once!"

"Yes," another agreed. "Let's go to see the Messiah the Lord has promised!"

All the shepherds were very excited. They entered Bethlehem and found the stable. Looking inside, they saw everything exactly as the angel had told them.

With shy smiles, the shepherds drew close and knelt down before the baby lying in the manger.

One of them said to Mary, "We are only poor shepherds. Thank you for letting us see this special child."

Mary looked first at the cooing baby Jesus and then at the shepherds. "Jesus is born for all of us," Mary told them. "Thank *you* for visiting us in such a simple stable."

The shepherds told Mary and Joseph all that the angels had said. When they left, the shepherds were full of joy.

"Praise the Lord, who has done such marvelous deeds!" cried out one of the shepherds.

"The Messiah has truly come!" said another. "We must spread the good news!"

The shepherds weren't the only ones to notice the new star. Three wise men had also seen it, and they knew that it announced the birth of the king of the Jews. These Magi, who came from countries east of Israel, had decided to worship this newborn king. Riding on their tall camels, they had followed the star over many miles of barren desert.

Now passing through the gates of Bethlehem, Gaspar
called out to the two men behind him. "Balthasar!
Melchior! I believe we are nearing our destination."

"It does appear that the star is directly over that spot,"
Melchior agreed, pointing.

The three men rode on until they reached a stable.

"Where is the palace?" Balthasar wondered. "Surely a king would be born in a palace."

"But this is where the star has led us," said Melchior. "We've come so far. . . . Let's go in."

The Magi expected to find only a stable full of sleeping animals. But as they dismounted from their camels, they heard a woman's voice.

"Hush," the quiet voice said, "it's time to close your eyes and go to sleep."

The only response the Magi heard was the happy gurgle of a baby.

"Perhaps the king *is* here," whispered Gaspar.

The three men unloaded the packs the camels carried and went into the stable. Although all around Bethlehem people were sleeping, the Magi found a man and a woman holding a baby. Animals gathered around them, keeping the family warm.

Melchior cleared his throat and said, "Pardon us for disturbing you, but we have traveled a great distance to come and honor this new king."

Joseph put his arm around Mary and Jesus. He said, "Please, come closer. This is Jesus. We have little to offer you, but you are most welcome."

The Magi came closer and knelt in adoration before Jesus.

"We have each brought gifts," said Melchior. "I bring the King of kings the gift of gold."

Gaspar opened his gift and a sweet smell filled the stable. "I bring the King who is also God the gift of frankincense."

"And I," said Balthasar, "bring the gift of myrrh to the King and Savior of all people."

Baby Jesus looked at the three men. Then the smiling child reached for them as if to bless them.

When the Magi left, Mary drew closer to her sleepy
Son in the manger. "I love you, my child," she whispered.
"It's time to close your eyes now." As Jesus drifted
off to sleep, and Joseph laid down some fresh hay for
the animals, Mary thought about everything that had
happened. Then, looking at her peaceful baby, Mary
prayed, "Whatever the future holds, Lord, I will always
thank you for the greatest gift you could have ever given
me, for the greatest gift this world will ever know: Jesus."

Sister Marlyn Evangelina Monge has been a Daughter of St. Paul since 2005 and currently serves as an editor for books for children and teens at Pauline Books & Media. Before entering the convent, she taught bilingual kindergarten for six years, taught in her parish's religious education program, and volunteered with the youth ministry program.

Sister Marlyn has a master's degree in education and enjoys finding ways to help children discover the wealth of their faith through the stories she writes and edits. She is the author of many books for children, including the award-winning *Jorge de Argentina*. Sister Marlyn is a proud *tía* (aunt) to her six nieces and nephews.

Lisa M. Griffin is an illustrator specializing in stories for children. She has illustrated over a dozen books including her first creative adventure as an author/illustrator with *Hey Goose! What's Your Excuse?* She holds a bachelor of fine arts in Illustration and is a member of The Society of Children's Book Writers and Illustrators.

Lisa spends most days in her cozy New Hampshire studio enjoying a warm cup of tea while sketching and working on picture books. When she isn't drawing and daydreaming, Lisa enjoys reading, yoga, photography, and spending time with her family.

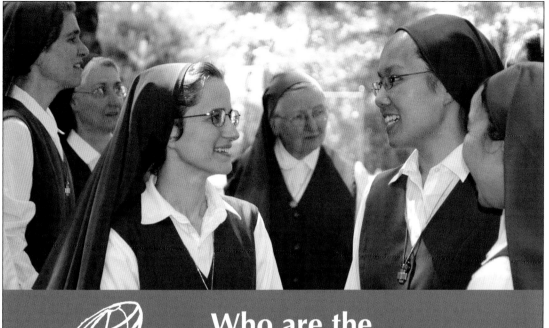

Who are the Daughters of St. Paul?

We are Catholic sisters with a mission. Our task is to bring the love of Jesus to everyone like Saint Paul did. You can find us in over 50 countries. Our founder, Blessed James Alberione, showed us how to reach out to the world through the media. That's why we publish books, make movies and apps, record music, broadcast on radio, perform concerts, help people at our bookstores, visit parishes, host JClub book fairs, use social media and the Internet, and pray for all of you.

BOOKS & MEDIA

The Daughters of St. Paul operate book and media centers at the following addresses. Visit, call, or write the one nearest you today, or find us at www.paulinestore.org.

CALIFORNIA
3908 Sepulveda Blvd, Culver City, CA 90230   310-397-8676
3250 Middlefield Road, Menlo Park, CA 94025   650-369-4230

FLORIDA
145 SW 107th Avenue, Miami, FL 33174   305-559-6715

HAWAII
1143 Bishop Street, Honolulu, HI 96813   808-521-2731

ILLINOIS
172 North Michigan Avenue, Chicago, IL 60601   312-346-4228

LOUISIANA
4403 Veterans Memorial Blvd, Metairie, LA 70006   504-887-7631

MASSACHUSETTS
885 Providence Hwy, Dedham, MA 02026   781-326-5385

MISSOURI
9804 Watson Road, St. Louis, MO 63126   314-965-3512

NEW YORK
115 E. 29th Street, New York City, NY 10016   212-754-1110

SOUTH CAROLINA
243 King Street, Charleston, SC 29401   843-577-0175

TEXAS
No book center; for parish exhibits or outreach evangelization, contact:
210-569-0500 or SanAntonio@paulinemedia.com or P.O. Box 761416,
San Antonio, TX 78245

VIRGINIA
1025 King Street, Alexandria, VA 22314   703-549-3806

CANADA
3022 Dufferin Street, Toronto, ON M6B 3T5   416-781-9131